THE BIG LITTLE BOOK OF

Irish Wit & Wisdom

THE BIG LITTLE BOOK OF
Irish
Wit & Wisdom

SIX VOLUMES IN ONE

Irish Blessings

Irish Toasts

Irish Proverbs

Irish Riddles

Irish Laws

Irish Wisdom

BLACK DOG
& LEVENTHAL
PUBLISHERS
NEW YORK

This edition published by arrangement with Chronicle Books,
San Francisco, CA

Pages 365 and 366 constitute an extension of this copyright page.

Published by **Black Dog & Leventhal Publishers, Inc.**

151 West 19th Street, New York, NY 10011

Distributed by **Workman Publishing Company**

708 Broadway, New York, NY 10003

Printed and bound in Italy

a c e g i j h f d b

ISBN: 1-884822-73-8

Library of Congress Cataloging-in-Publication Data
The Big little book of Irish wit & wisdom : six volumes in one.
p.   cm.
The six books were originally published separately: San Francisco,
Calif. : Chronicle Books, 1986–1994.
Contents: Irish blessings — Irish laws — Irish proverbs —
Irish riddles — Irish toasts — Irish wisdom.
ISBN 1-884822-73-8
1. Irish wit and humor.   2. Ireland — Literary collections.
PN6178.I6854   1997
820.8'09415 — dc21   97-22557
CIP

Contents

Irish Blessings 7

Irish Toasts 67

Irish Proverbs 125

Irish Riddles 185

Irish Laws 245

Irish Wisdom 305

PAT FAIRON

IRISH BLESSINGS

ILLUSTRATED BY *Joanna Martin*

Introduction

This little collection of prayers and blessings is drawn from the oral traditions of a people who saw God's handiwork in everything about them. Livelihood and life itself was seen as being dependent on God's will. It was only natural, therefore, to ask for His divine help in every aspect of daily life. This impulse is the origin of these simple and beautiful little prayers and blessings.

Pat Fairon
Loughgall, Co. Armagh

For Father and Mother

For my mother who raised me at her breast
And for my father who raised me
by the work of his bones;
I trust in the Son of God when
they enter his presence
That there will be a hundred thousand
welcomes for them
In the heavens of peace.

On Awakening

May God and the Virgin Mary, who have
brought myself and my children from the
sleep of death last night to the brightness of
today, bring us safe from all danger and
deliver us from the enemy of both body
and soul.

On Hearing the Cock Crow

"May the light of the sun shine
on us today" say we,
"The son of the virgin is safe"
says the cock,
"Rise up, woman of the house
and get the fire going".

On Seeing the Sun

O God who created the sun, You are the sun
of my soul and I adore Your brightness.
I love You, O Everlasting Light. May I see
You in the bright light of Your glory.

. . .

O king of brightness and the sun
Who knows our worth,
Be with us every day,
Be with us every night,
Be with us every night and day,
Be with us every day and night.

Lighting the Fire

I will light my fire today
In the presence of the holy, heavenly angels,
In the presence of Gabriel
Most beautiful of form,
In the presence of Urial of all beauty,
Without hatred, without envy, without jealousy,
Without fear, without dread of
Anything under the sun,
And with the Holy Son of God as my refuge.
Lord, kindle in my innermost heart
The ember of love
For My enemies, for my relatives,
for my friends,
For the wise, for the foolish, for the wretched.

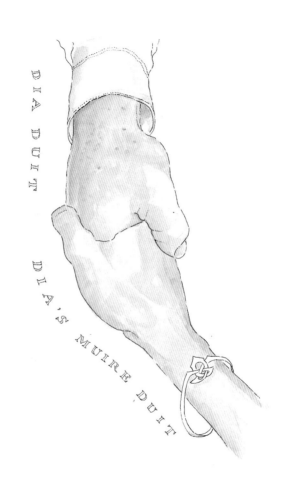

DIA DUIT

DIA'S MUIRE DUIT

A Greeting

Greeting: God greet you.

Reply: God and Mary greet you

or

God, Mary and Patrick greet you

. . .

In Gaelic

Greeting: Dia duit

Reply: Dia's Muire duit

Going Out and About

The belt of Christ about me on my going out
and on my coming in

·　　·　　·

In the name of God who made a pathway of
the waves,
May He bring us safely home at the end of
the day.

·　　·　　·

God be on your road every way you go.

Before Work

May God bless the work.

• • •

Let's begin in the name of God.

Ending Work

The blessings of God on the souls of the dead,
And may the great God grant us life and health,
And may he prosper our work and
the work of Christians.

Making Bread

The grace of God and the favour of Patrick
on all that I see and all that I do.
The blessing that God put on the five loaves
and two fishes, may He put on this food.

Prayer on Milking a Cow

The blessings of Mary and the blessing of God,
The blessing of the Sun
And the Moon in her road
Of the man in the East and the
Man in the West,
And my blessings be with thee
And be thou blest.

Charm against Backache

May Peter take it and take it Paul,
May Michael take it and take it John,
May Moleesha take it, may Mweelin take
This pain from my back, this savage ache.

Blessing the Cow

The blessing of God on you, cow,
And twice as many blessings on your calf.
Come, Mary, and sit,
Come, Brigid, and milk,
Come, Holy Michael Archangel
And bless the beef,
In the name of the Father, Son
and Holy Spirit.

A Mother's Blessing on a Son or Daughter Leaving Home

The great God between
Your two shoulder blades
To protect you in your going and returning,
The Son of the Virgin Mary
Be close to your heart,
And the perfect Holy Spirit
Be keeping an eye on you.

Going to Sea or Crossing a River

Going over the deep place,
O God of patience, take them by the hand
In case of a blow from a strong wave.
O Mary, look out for them
And don't leave them.

Grace before Meals

Bless us, O Lord,
Bless our food and drink,
You Who has so dearly redeemed us
And has saved us from evil,
As You have given us this share of food,
May You give us our share of the everlasting
glory.

Grace after Meals

Praise to the King of Plenty,
Praise every time to God,
A hundred praises and thanks to Jesus Christ,
For what we have eaten and shall eat.

Drinking a Health

We will drink this drink
As Patrick would drink it,
Full of grace and spilling over,
Without fighting or quarrelling or hint of shame,
Or knowing that we will last until tomorrow.
We ask the help of our Mother Mary,
For she is our support at all times,
This is our toast to all here present
And may the Son of Grace be helping us.

Going through a Graveyard

God greet you, all gathered here,
May God and Mary greet you.
As we are now so once were you,
As you are now so shall we be.
May all of us prosper under
The bright King of the world.

Taking Snuff at a Wake

Seven fills of Patrick's Island,
Seven fills of the tomb of Christ,
Of the blessings of the good God
on your soul,
And on the souls of the seven generations
before you.

Three Folds in my Garment

Three folds in my garment
Yet only one garment I bear
Three joints in a finger
Yet only one finger is there
Three leaves in a shamrock
Yet only one shamrock I wear
Frost, ice and snow
Yet these three are nothing but water
Three persons in God
Yet only one God is there

Prayers for the Dead

God be good to their souls
God rest them
God rest their souls
God have mercy on them.

Putting a Child to Sleep

May God bless you, child.
I put you under the protection of Mary
and her Son,
Under the care of Brigid and her cloak,
And under the shelter of God tonight.

Banking the Fire

I preserve this fire as Christ has
preserved everyone.
Mary on the roof ridge, Brigid in the middle,
And the eight most powerful angels
in the City of Grace
Protect this house and this hearth
and safeguard its people.

. . .

Let us bank this fire in honour
of Holy Patrick.
May our house not be burnt or
our people murdered,
And may the bright sun of tomorrow shine
on us all, at home or abroad.

I Make this Bed Tonight

In the name of the Father, the Son
and the Holy Spirit,
In the name of the night we were begot,
In the name of the day we were baptised,
In the name of each and every saint and apostle
That is in Heaven

For a Happy Death

When your eyes shall be closing
And your mouth be opening
And your senses be slipping away.
When your heart shall grow cold
And your limbs be old
God comfort your soul that day.

Lighting the Light

Saviour, may You give heavenly light to every poor soul that has left this world and to every poor soul we wish to pray for.

Putting Out the Light

May God not put out the light of Heaven on our soul or on the souls of the dead who are gone before us with the sign of faith.

On Seeing the New Moon

On this saint's day which has brought in this new moon, as we are in good health at its coming, may we be in good health when it goes and when it comes again.

(Said standing when one sees the new moon)

On Lying Down

I lie down with my dear God,
May my dear God lie with me,
The two hands of God about my waist,
A cross of angels over me
From head to sole,
Tonight and until a year from tonight,
And tonight itself.

A Blessing on Everyone

As plentiful as the grass that grows,
Or the sand on the shore,
Or the dew on the lea,
So the blessings of the King of Grace
On every soul that was, that is, or will be.

The Emigrant's Prayer

Brigid that is in Faughart,
Blinne that is in Killeavey,
Bronagh that is in Ballinakill,
May you bring me back to Ireland.

(Title page illustration)

IRISH TOASTS

ILLUSTRATED BY *Karen Bailey*

Sláinte!

'In my young days, when two or three men went in for a drink together, it was the custom for them to go into a back room — a snug. They never stood at the counter. Each of them would strike three hefty blows on the table and, in a flash, the barmaid would be in to see what they wanted. She would be ordered to bring them a half-pint of whiskey and, in due course, she would return with a jug and a glass. Should there be ten men in the company, they would still only have the one glass. The man who had ordered and paid for the drink would then stand up and hand a glass of whiskey to the man nearest to him, who would then say 'Here's health' (*Seo do shláinte*) to which the first man might answer, 'God grant you health' (*Sláinte ó Dhia duit*). That's the kind of toast they used to drink and it was always with a blow of the ash plant that they summoned the barman or barmaid.'

NIALL Ó DUBHTHAIGH

May you be poor in misfortune,
Rich in blessings,
Slow to make enemies,
Quick to make friends.
But rich or poor, quick or slow,
May you know nothing
but happiness
From this day forward.

May the face of every good news
And the back of every bad news
Be towards us.

Like the goodness of the five
loaves and two fishes,
Which God divided among the five
thousand men,
May the blessing of the King
who so divided
Be upon our share of this
common meal!

May the road rise to meet you
May the wind be always
at your back
The sun shine warm upon your face
The rain fall soft upon your fields
And until we meet again
May God hold you in the hollow
of His hand.

May the roof above us never fall in,
And may we friends gathered below
Never fall out.

May you have food and raiment,
A soft pillow for your head,
May you be forty years in heaven
Before the devil knows you're dead!

The health of all Ireland
and of County Mayo,
And when that much is dead,
may we still be on the go;
From the County of Meath,
the health of the hag,
Not of her but her drink
is the reason we brag;
Your health one and all,
from one wall to the other,
And, you outside there —
speak up, brother!

May the strength of three
be in your journey.

May peace and plenty be the first
To lift the latch on your door,
And happiness be guided
to your home
By the candle of Christmas.

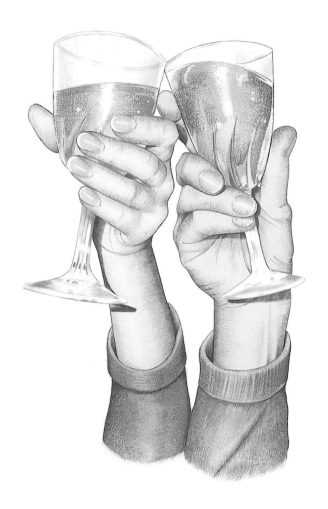

In the New Year, may your right
hand always
Be stretched out in friendship
and never in want.

St Patrick was a gentleman
Who through strategy and stealth
Drove all the snakes from Ireland,
Here's a toasting to his health;
But not too many toastings
Lest you lose yourself and then
Forget the good St Patrick
And see all those snakes again.

May there be a fox on your
fishing-hook
And a hare on your bait
And may you kill no fish
Until St Brigid's Day.

The health of the salmon
and of the trout
That swim back and forward near
the Bull's Mouth;
Don't ask for saucepan, jug or mug,
Down the hatch — drink it up!

Here's to you and yours
and to mine and ours,
And if mine and ours ever come
across you and yours,
I hope you and yours will do
as much for mine and ours,
As mine and ours have done
for you and yours!

May you have warm words
on a cold evening,
A full moon on a dark night,
And the road downhill all the way
to your door.

May there be a generation
of children
On the children of your children.

Here's that we may always have
A clean shirt
A clean conscience
And a guinea in our pocket.

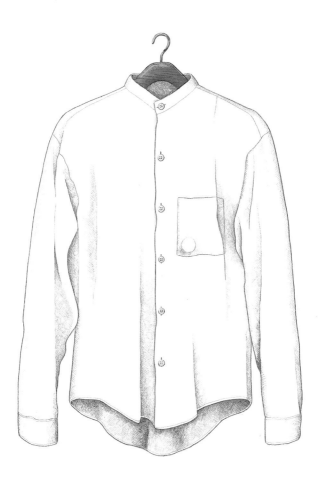

Here's a health
To your enemies' enemies!

Here's health and prosperity,
To you and all your posterity,
And them that doesn't drink
with sincerity,
That they may be damned
for all eternity!

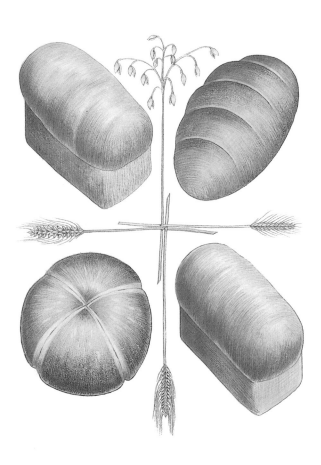

Rye bread will do you good,
Barley bread will do you no harm,
Wheaten bread will sweeten
your blood,
Oaten bread will strengthen
your arm.

May you live to be
a hundred years,
With one extra year to repent.

May I see you grey
And combing your children's hair.

Health and long life to you
The woman of your choice to you
A child every year to you
Land without rent to you
And may you die in Ireland.

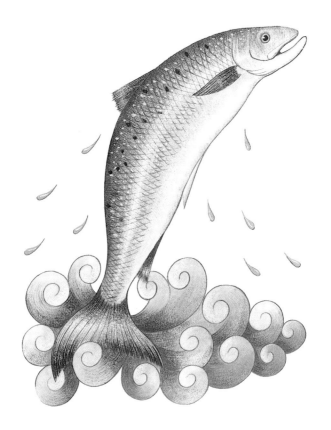

The health of the salmon to you,
A long life,
A full heart
And a wet mouth.

May the grass grow long
On the road to hell
For want of use.

May the Lord keep you
in His hand
And never close His fist too tight
on you.

Saint Brigid's Prayer

from the Irish

I'd like to give a lake of beer to God.
I'd love the Heavenly
Host to be tippling there
For all eternity.

I'd love the men of Heaven to live with me,
To dance and sing.
If they wanted, I'd put at their disposal
Vats of suffering.

White cups of love I'd give them
With a heart and a half;
Sweet pitchers of mercy I'd offer
To every man.

I'd make Heaven a cheerful spot
Because the happy heart is true.
I'd make the men contented for their own sake.
I'd like Jesus to love me too.

I'd like the people of Heaven to gather
From all the parishes around.
I'd give a special welcome to the women,
The three Marys of great renown.

I'd sit with the men, the women and God
There by the lake of beer.
We'd be drinking good health forever
And every drop would be a prayer.

BRENDAN KENNELLY

IRISH PROVERBS

ILLUSTRATED BY *Karen Bailey*

*what's good for the goose
is good for the gander.*

The older the fiddle
the sweeter the tune

It's no use boiling
your cabbage twice

There's no need to
fear the wind
if your haystacks are
tied down

Do not mistake
a goat's beard for
a fine stallion's tail

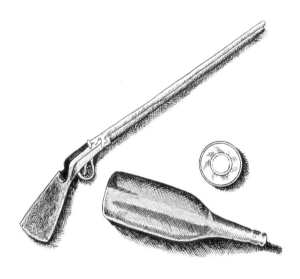

Drink is the curse of the land·
It makes you fight with
your neighbour · It makes
you shoot at your landlord~
and it makes you miss him

If you lie down with dogs
you'll rise with fleas

A wild goose never
reared a tame gosling

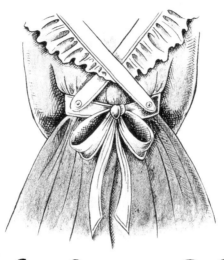

A boy's best friend is his
mother & there's no
spancel stronger than
her apron string

There never was an
OLD SLIPPER
but there was an
OLD STOCKING
to match it

Firelight will not let you
read fine stories but it's
warm & you won't see the
dust on the floor.

As the old cock crows
the young cock learns

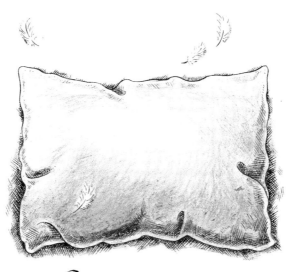

Humour, to a man,
is like a feather pillow.
It is filled with what is
easy to get but gives
great comfort

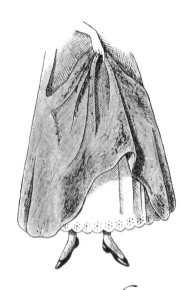

Many an Irish property
was increased by the lace
of a daughter's petticoat

The best way to keep loyalty
in a mans heart is to keep
money in his purse

A narrow neck keeps the
bottle from being emptied
in one swig

A trout in the pot
is better than
a salmon in the sea

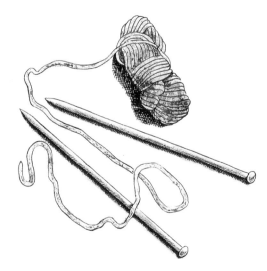

If the knitter is weary
the baby
will have no new bonnet

Its for her own good
that the cat purrs

Even a tin knocker
will shine on a dirty door

An old broom knows
the dirty corners best

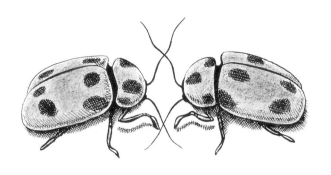

one beetle
recognizes another

To the raven
her own chick is white

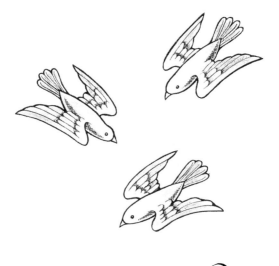

When the sky falls
we'll all catch larks

Any man can lose
his hat in a fairy-wind

If you have one pair of
good soles it's better than
two pairs of good uppers

It's no use carrying an
UMBRELLA
if your shoes are leaking

It's difficult to choose
between two blind goats

A silent mouth is
sweet to hear

It's as hard to see a
woman crying as it is to
see a barefooted duck

He'd offer you an egg if
you promised not to
break the shell

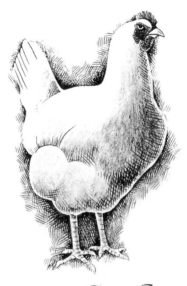

It's a bad hen
that won't scratch herself

No matter how often a
pitcher goes to the water
it is broken in the end

There was never a
scabby sheep in a flock
that didn't like to have
a comrade

A nod is as good as a wink
to a blind horse

The fox never found a
better messenger than
himself

There'll be
WHITE · BLACKBIRDS
before an unwilling woman
ties the knot

Show the fatted calf but
not the thing that
fattened him

A buckle is a great
addition to an old shoe

In winter the milk
goes to the cow's horns

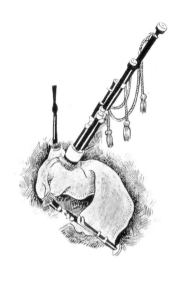

Men are like bagpipes:
no sound comes from them
till they're full

Snuff at a wake is fine
if there's nobody sneezing
over the snuff box

You must crack the nuts
before
you can eat the kernel

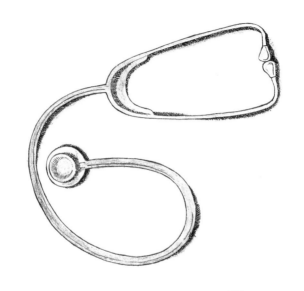

Every patient is a doctor
after his cure

Neither give cherries to
pigs nor advice to a fool

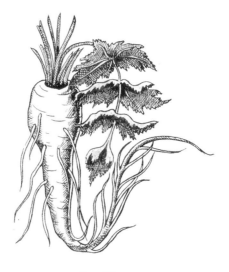

Soft words butter no
parsnips but they won't
harden the heart of the
cabbage either.

You'll never plough a field
by turning it over in
your mind

There are
FINER · FISH
in the sea
than have ever been
CAUGHT

A Tyrone woman will
never buy a rabbit
without a head
for fear its a cat

A windy day is
not the day for thatching

The old pipe gives
the sweetest smoke

Marriages are all happy
It's having breakfast
together that causes all
the trouble

*A scholar's ink
lasts longer than
a martyr's blood*

8

Take gifts with a sigh,
most men give to be paid

DECEMBER
25

A turkey never voted
for an early Christmas

what butter & whiskey
will not cure
there's no cure for

The Irish forgive their
great men when they are
safely buried

The longest road out
is the shortest road home

PAT FAIRON

IRISH RIDDLES

ILLUSTRATED BY *Philip Blythe*

Introduction

In an oral tradition true riddles seem to offer a playful challenge to the people's conventional views of their world. They do this by describing the familiar in words and terms that make it sound magical and mysterious. Unlike other forms of the riddle, true riddles aim not to trick or puzzle but to offer a fresh view of the world. To me they are poems – peoples' poetry.

Pat Fairon
Loughgall, Co. Armagh
1992

Answers
Answers to the riddles are on page 244

A steel pig going over a bone bridge
and a brass man driving it.

EST. 1921   S. EWING. & SONS

PHILIP BLYTHE '72

It was in the river but wasn't drowned
It was in the grass but wasn't cut
It was in the shop but wasn't sold.

As white as milk but milk it's not
As green as grass but grass it's not
As red as a rose but rose it's not.
As black as ink but ink it's not.

PHILIP BLYTHE '92.

Who do I see coming through the sea
But the toy of the sun
A man with a blue coat
And a red thread in his shirt.

Big biddy from the north
Has a big mouth but can't talk
Two iron ears and can't hear
Three iron legs and can't walk.

It once was low
But now it's high
It once was wet
But now it's dry
It once was black
But now it's red
I put it upstanding
And it fell down dead.

Two brothers we are, great burdens
we bear
In which we are bitterly pressed
The truth we do speak, we are full
all the day
And empty when we go to rest.

When I'm old they cut me
And in a hole they put me
When I'm three months old
They come looking me quite bold
Between fire and water they
burn me
Between two irons they turn me
And when I'm stripped of my skin
They find a hole to put me in.

Hidi Hadi on the wall
Hidi Hadi got a fall
Three men and threescore
Wouldn't leave Hidi Hadi
As he was before.

A hopper o' ditches
A cropper o' corn

A wee brown cow
And a pair of leather horns.

Through a rock, through a reel
Through an old spinning wheel
Through a bag of feathers
Through an old mud wall
If that's not a riddle
There's no riddle at all.

Brothers and sisters have I none
But this man's father
Was my father's son.

Who is it?

I washed my face in water
That was never rained or run
I dried it with a towel
That was neither wove nor spun.

PHILIP BOSHE 92

In a marble hall
As white as milk
Lined with a skin
As soft as silk
Within a fountain
Crystal clear
A golden apple doth appear
No doors there are to this
stronghold
Yet thieves break in to steal
the gold.

A bannock of bread
And a sheet full of crumbs.

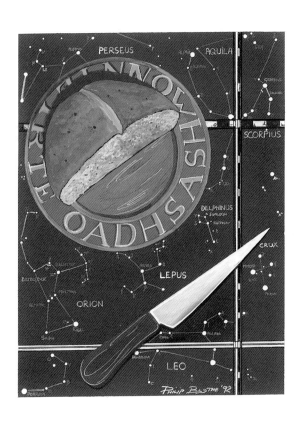

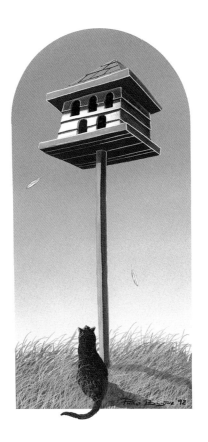

A house full
A room full
And couldn't catch
A spoonful.

Two legs on the ground
And three legs overhead
And the head of the living
In the mouth of the dead.

Neither fish nor flesh
Nor feathers nor bone
But still has fingers
And thumbs of its own.

As I went through yon guttery gap
I met a wee man in gay red cap
A stick in his stern and a stone
in his belly
Riddle me that and I'll give
you a penny.

Hink! Hank! On the bank
Ten drawing four.

A hard-working father
And an easygoing mother
Twelve little children
As black as one another.

As black as ink
As white as milk
And hops on the road
Like hailstone.

As round as an apple
As deep as a pail
She'll never bawl out
Till she's caught by the tail.

Hicky Picky locked the gate
Hicky Picky locked it weel
Hicky Picky locked the gate
Without iron or steel!

Four steady standards
Four diddle diddle danders
Two lookers, two hookers
And a wig-wag.

Philip Blythe '92

Patch upon patch
Without any stitches
Riddle me that
And I'll buy you some britches.

Long head
Crooked thighs
A wee head
And no eyes!

It ate everything that came
And everything that will
And still it'll never get its fill.

Answers

p.4	A needle and a finger with a thimble
p.7	The sun
p.8	A blackberry
p.11	A rainbow
p.12	A pot
p.15	A sod of turf
p.16	A pair of boots
p.19	A potato
p.20	A broken egg
p.23	A hare
p.24	A moth
p.27	Oneself
p.28	Wash in the dew Dry in the sun
p.31	An egg
p.32	The moon and the stars
p.35	Smoke
p.36	A man with his head in a pot
p.39	A glove
p.40	A haw
p.43	A man milking a cow
p.44	A clock face
p.47	A magpie
p.48	A bell
p.51	Frost
p.52	A cow
p.55	A cabbage
p.56	The tongs
p.59	A graveyard

COMPILED BY

MARY DOWLING DALEY

IRISH LAWS

ILLUSTRATED BY *Ian McCullough*

Introduction

Passed on orally from at least the first century BC the Brehon Laws, named for Ireland's wandering jurists, were first set down on parchment in the seventh century AD, using the newly-developed, written Irish language, and continued in use until the beginning of the seventeenth century.

Although the Irish had been living by the laws since before the time of Julius Caesar, by the time of Elizabeth I the Brehons, along with the Irish poets, were considered a danger to the realm, and the old laws 'lewd', 'unreasonable', and 'barbarous'. And so the Brehons, the poets and the ancient laws were banned and English common law substituted. It was the end of the Gaelic order.

Some of the Brehons buried their precious manuscripts, or hid them behind loose stones in the hearth. Other manuscripts became torn or damp, and were burned or allowed to rot. Fortunately, a good number of manuscripts fell into the hands of collectors, and are now safe in the libraries of Trinity College and the Royal Irish Academy in Dublin, at the British Museum, Oxford University and on the continent of Europe.

In 1852 the Brehon Law Commission employed two

native Irish scholars, Eugene O'Curry and John O'Donovan, to unravel the mysteries of the laws. For years they poured over the manuscripts. Sitting in dimly-lit libraries, surrounded by pens and ink-pots, every day they peered through magnifying glasses at the handwriting of the old scribes, struggling to decipher the tiny glosses that ran between the lines and up the margins. For clarity they first copied the laws onto fresh sheets of paper. Then they translated them into English.

What gradually came to light as, in the words of D. A. Binchy, 'the crabbed and obscure texts. . . yielded up their secrets', was not simply a collection of dry and dusty prohibitions, but thousands of details – details that describe ancient life in the days when the Irish still lived in mud huts and small ringed settlements, and paid their bills in cows and bacon, handsome gold brooches and ordinary wooden bowls: the brewer testing a grain of malt against his tooth to guard against bitterness in the ale; farmers lugging sides of beef to the chieftain, to pay their quarterly rent; a pregnant wife who craves a morsel of food; mischievous boys shouting at pigs.

Myles Dillon has called the Irish law-tracts 'probably the most important documents of their kind in the whole tradition of western Europe.' The value lies not only in their great antiquity, or in the pictures of everyday life unavailable from other sources. It may lie primarily in the fact that the Irish Celts, unlike those of France and Britain, were never conquered by Rome. Instead, Ireland had grown up in what some like to call 'splendid isolation' across the Irish sea.

So the Irish laws serve as a repository of primitive customs, some dating back 3,000 years and most gathered by Celtic wanderers from various members of the far-flung Indo-European family.

Certain Irish laws, for example, mirror the Germanic tribal custom of demanding payment of a fine, generally in livestock, for deliberate assault or homicide. Others outline preparations for the great assemblies held regularly at Tara and other pagan burial sites long before the arrival of Patrick – gatherings that correspond to the assemblies and funeral games held at the Roman Forum. Scholars could conceivably compare the strong position of women in the Irish laws with that of women in Greece at the time of Homer.

Perhaps the Hindu procedure of sitting *dharna* most dramatically reveals the ancient Indo-European connections: a creditor, particularly one of a lower class than the recalcitrant debtor, was entitled to sit in front of the debtor's house daily and fast, to embarrass the debtor into paying up.

Other laws, such as the Irish 'blush-fine' for unjustly satirizing a fellow tribesman, demonstrate the dread of losing face, a fear shared with the ancient Irish by such widely scattered societies as the Japanese, and the Ashanti tribespeople of Ghana. Moreover, the Brehon Laws often remind Jews of the *Talmud*, and other scholars of pre-Islamic Arab traditions.

Although scholars have called the old Irish laws 'gravely defective' in that they were not based on principles or never produced a central organization, Eoin MacNeill wrote in 1934 that even Ireland's enemies in the time of Elizabeth and James I commented on the love of the Irish for justice, and for their laws. I, for one, can see why.

THE GREAT TRIBAL ASSEMBLY AT CARMAN

The Feis

'There they discussed and debated
the rights and taxes of the province:
every legal enactment right piously,
every third year it was settled.'

from *The Poem of Carman*

(11th century)

Every third year roads must be cleared of brambles, weeds and water to prepare for the great assembly.

The harpist is the only musician
who is of noble standing.
Flute-players, trumpeters and timpanists,
as well as jugglers, conjurers and equestrians who
stand on the backs of horses at fairs, have no status
of their own in the community, only that of the noble
chieftain to whom they are attached.

The creditor who holds your brooch, your necklet
or your earrings as a pledge against your loan must
return them so you may wear them
at the great assembly.

Or he will be fined for your humiliation.

Speech is given to three:
to the historian-poet for the narration
and relating of tales,
to the poet-seer for praise and satire,
and to the Brehon for giving judgement.

The time allotted to each Brehon for pleading his case
is long or short according to his dignity.
In determining the length of the speech he is allowed,
count eighteen breathings to the minute.

When a judge deviates from the truth a blotch
will appear on his cheek.

On the best land everything is good. The herbs are
sweet and no manure or shells are needed. There will
be no plants that will stick in a horse's mane or tail:
no briars, no blackthorns, no burdocks.

For the best arable land the price is twenty-four cows.
The price for dry, coarse land is twelve dry cows.

How many things add to the price of land?
A wood, a mine, the site of a mill, a highway, a road,
a great sea, a river, a mountain, a river falling
into the sea, a cooling pond for cattle.
Add three cows to the price if it is near a chieftain's
house or a monastery.

For stripping the bark of an oak tree, enough to tan
the leather for a pair of woman's shoes,
the fine is one cow-hide.
The defendant must cover the bruised portion with
a mixture of wet clay, new milk and cow-dung.

If a man takes a woman off on a horse, into the woods or onto a sea-going ship, and if members of the woman's tribe are present, they must object within twenty-four hours or they may not demand payment of the fine.

The husband-to-be shall pay a bride-price of land,
cattle, horses, gold or silver to the father of the bride.
Husband and wife retain individual rights to
all the land, flocks and household goods
each brings to the marriage.

The husband who, through listlessness, does not go
to his wife in her bed must pay a fine.

If a pregnant woman craves a morsel of food and
her husband withholds it through stinginess
or neglect, he must pay a fine.

Children shall be sent at an early age to distant
members of the tribe to be reared in the hereditary
professions of law, medicine, poetic composition
or war, or of tilling the soil and wifeliness.
Foster children shall be returned to their parents
at the marriage age: fourteen for girls
and seventeen for boys.

If a woman makes an assignation with a man to come
to her in a bed or behind a bush, the man is not
considered guilty even if she screams.
If she has not agreed to a meeting, however,
he is guilty as soon as she screams.

If the chief wife scratches the concubine but it is out
of rightful jealousy that she does it,
she is exempt from liability for injury.
The same does not hold true for injuries
by the concubine.

Six cows are the fine for breaking a tribesman's
two front teeth; twelve heifers, for maiming
a homeless man.
For pulling off the hairs of a virgin bishop the fine
is one yearling heifer for every twenty hairs.

The doctor shall build his house over a running stream.
His house must not be slovenly or smeared
with the tracks of snails.
It must have four doors that open out so the patients
may be seen from every side at all times.

No fools, drunks or female scolds are allowed in the
doctor's house when a patient is healing there. No bad
news to be brought, and no talking across the bed.
No grunting of pigs or barking of dogs outside.

If the doctor heals your wound, but it breaks out anew
because of his carelessness, neglect or gross want
of skill, he must return the fee you paid.
He must also pay you damages as if he himself
had wounded you.

Whoever comes to your door, you must feed him
or care for him, with no questions asked.

It is illegal to give someone food in which has been found a dead mouse or weasel.

The chief poet of the tribe shall sit next to the king at a banquet. Each shall be served the choicest cut of meat.

The poet who overcharges for a poem shall be stripped of half his rank in society.

Cows, pigs, horses, sheep, goats,
dogs, cats, hens, geese – noisy goods!
Little bees that stick to all flowers.
These are the ten beasts
of all the world's men.
(The Chieftain who is keeper of the free public hostel
must have one hundred of all of these.)

The hostel-keeper must own a cauldron large enough
to boil a pig and a cow at the same time.
Before taking the meat out of the boiling cauldron
the attendant must warn, 'Stand back – here goes the
fleshfork into the cauldron!'

A layman may drink six pints of ale with his dinner, but a monk may drink only three pints. This is so he will not be intoxicated when prayer-time arrives.

The feller of trees must warn all within shouting
distance before he takes the first blow.
All beasts, blind persons and people dozing
must be removed from the area.

If an accident occurs while a building is under
construction no fine is due for injury to the bystander
who is present only out of curiosity.
Should the owners of the building have knowledge
of danger or defect, however, full payment shall be
made to those present on legitimate business,
and to beasts.
(But only half payment to idlers.)

The blacksmith must rouse all sleeping customers
before he puts the iron in the fire.
This is to guard against injuries by sparks.
*Those who fall asleep again will receive
no compensation for injuries.*

If the head of the blacksmith's hammer flies off
the handle and injures a customer, neither the smith
nor the striker of the hammer is liable – *unless they
knew the head was loose.*

If a chip of wood from the carpenter's axe hits
a bystander the carpenter is exempt from liability
unless he deliberately aimed the chip at the bystander.

The mill-owner is exempt from liability for injury
to a person caught between the mill-stones.

If your land has neither fence nor stone wall
you must restrain your beasts lest they damage
your neighbour's property.
For goats a shoe of leather goes on each leg,
for yearling calves put on a spancel. The pig,
which does the most damage of all, must wear a yoke.

The fine for the hen's trespass into the neighbour's
herb garden is one oat-cake plus a side-dish
of butter or bacon.
To keep your hen at home you shall tie a withe
around her feet.

If your neighbour does not repay the debt
he owes you, you may prevent him from going
about his daily business.
A withe-tie (for all to see) goes on the blacksmith's
anvil, the carpenter's axe or the tree-feller's hatchet.
He is on his honour to do no work until he has
righted the wrong.

If the poet or the physician is in debt, immobilize
his horse-whip, for both ride their circuits
on the backs of horses.

Five-fold are crimes:
the crime of the hand, by wounding or stealing;
the crime of the foot, by kicking or moving
to do evil deeds;
the crime of the tongue, by satire, slander
or false witness;
the crime of the mouth, by eating stolen things;
the crime of the eye, by watching while an evil deed
is taking place.

The fine for killing a bond-person held as security
for a loan (or for killing a slave) is twenty-one cows;
for killing a free farmer of Erin
the fine is forty-two cows.
For killing a noble the fine for homicide is paid,
plus an additional amount determined by
his rank in society.
Fines are doubled for malice aforethought.

For stealing your pigs or your sheep, for stripping
your herb garden, for wearing down your hatchet
or wood-axe, you may take your neighbour's
milk cows to the public animal pound for three days.
If he does not want his cows taken to the pound
for his crimes or his bad debts, he may give
his son as security instead.

Blush-fines are payable for insults offered to all
persons of every rank except the ne'er-do-well,
the squanderer, the selfish man who thinks only
of his cows and his fields (and not of other people),
the buffoon who distorts himself before crowds
at a fair and the professional satirist.

Notice of the hound in heat and the mad dog must be
sent to the four nearest neighbourhoods.

If a dog commits a nuisance on a neighbour's land the dog's ordure must be removed as far as its juice is found. The ground must be pressed and stamped upon by the heel, and fine clay put there to cover it. Compensation shall be paid in butter, dough or curds amounting to three times the size of the ordure.

The lender of a horse must give notice
of the horse's kicking habits.

Three days is the stay of your cattle in the pound
for a quarrel in the ale-house, injury of thy chief,
over-working a valuable horse, maiming thy chained
dog, disturbing a fair or a great assembly, or striking
or violating thy wife.

Five days for satirizing a man after his death.

If a youth incites a pig by shouting at it for sport,
and the pig charges at idlers in the farmyard,
the pig is exempt from liability for injuries.

February first is the day on which husband or wife
may decide to walk away from the marriage.

The fine for peering into your neighbour's house
without permission is one cow.
For taking a handful of straw off his thatched roof,
one calf is the penalty.

If a rational adult brings a simpleton into an ale-house just to amuse the patrons, and if the noise and excitement cause the simpleton to injure another patron, the adult who brought him there must make compensation.

If you see a horse straying near a river in the dark,
or a pit, and do nothing to save it,
you must make restitution.

When you become old your family must provide you
with one oatcake a day, plus a container of sour milk.
They must bathe you every twentieth night
and wash your head every Saturday.
Seventeen sticks of firewood is the allotment
for keeping you warm.

Notes

pages 287 and 288: a withe is a strip of flexible willow.

page 293: a blush-fine was a fine payable for causing embarrassment.

page 299: like concubinage, divorce was legal in Ireland until the twelfth century.

FERGUS KELLY

IRISH WISDOM

ILLUSTRATED BY *Aislinn Adams*

Introduction

The arrangement of ideas in groups of three is natural and convenient, and consequently we find examples of the triad form in practically all recorded literatures, both oral and written. Among the Celtic-speaking peoples, triads seem to have been particularly popular, and they feature prominently in the native oral traditions of Ireland, Scotland, Wales and Brittany. Many of these triads are witty, with an amusing climax – or anticlimax – in the third item. The technique can be illustrated by quoting a Scottish Gaelic triad of the last century: 'The three most pleasant things which ever happened to me: my mother, my home and my purse.'

In many Irish triads of the same period, there are humorous jibes at female behaviour – or in some cases at male inability to cope with it. Again, the third item may be an anticlimax, as in the following example: 'There are three kinds of men who fail to understand women: young men, old men and middle-aged men.' Mothers-in-law are the target of a triad recorded from oral tradition in many parts of Ireland: 'The three sharpest things in the world: the eye of a cat after a mouse, the eye of a mason after a stone, the eye of a mother-in-law after her daughter-in-law.'

Moving further back in time, we witness a similar rich tradition of triads in the early manuscripts of Ireland and Wales. The principal Welsh collection is found in thirteenth- and fourteenth-century manuscripts, but it contains triads which are many centuries older. The principal Irish collection – from which the present selection has been made – dates from about the ninth century. It contains 214 triads, as well as some duads (two items), tetrads (four items) and nonads (nine items). A translation of the complete collection was published by the great German scholar Kuno Meyer in 1906, but is long out of print. A new edition is in the course of preparation at the School of Celtic Studies, Dublin Institute for Advanced Studies.

Some of these triads may come from ninth-century oral tradition, but in general this is a literary composition, probably most of it the work of a single author. His aim is to describe various aspects of life as he sees it around him. Sometimes there is no implied moral in his observations: he is merely a neutral recorder of some natural or human phenomenon. But more often he adopts a particular ethical standpoint and uses the triad form to express his disapproval of vices, such as anger, lust, gluttony and laziness. He is especially concerned to castigate breaches of good manners or etiquette. We can thus learn from him how a person was expected to behave in polite society in ninth-century Ireland! In contrast to some of the triads of more recent folk tradition, his triads in general display respect for a woman's point of view. Indeed, one of the triads quoted in this selection encapsulates in a remarkably sympathetic and sensitive way the lot of a wife: 'Three drops of a married woman: a drop of blood, a tear-drop, a drop of sweat.'

Like many moralists, the author's observations are sometimes rather banal, but he can also be incisive and profound. He is particularly skilled at juxtaposing images from the natural world alongside some aspect of human behaviour, as in: 'Three wealths in barren places: a well in a mountain, fire out of a stone, wealth in the possession of a mean man.'

Technically, these triads display a number of interesting points. The triad which I have just quoted is an example of one of the author's favourite devices: the use of paradox. In this case, he is clearly fascinated by the paradox that two life-giving elements — water and fire — can reside in the seemingly lifeless environment of a mountain or a stone. He links these ideas with a further paradox: the wealthy man who is too mean to benefit anybody with his wealth. Another device which the author relishes is the arrangement of his triads in contrasting pairs. This feature can be seen in some of the triads in the present selection. For example, 'Three youthful sisters' is followed by 'Three aged sisters'.

I have no doubt that modern readers will find this well-chosen selection of Irish triads both entertaining and thought-provoking.

Fergus Kelly

Three things that are best in the world:

the hand of a good carpenter,
the hand of a skilled woman,
the hand of a good smith.

Three rejoicings followed by sorrow:

a wooer's,
a thief's,
a tale-bearer's.

Three rejoicings that are worse than sorrow:

the joy of a man who has defrauded another,
the joy of a man who has perjured himself,
the joy of a man who has slain his brother
in contesting his land.

Three unfortunate things for a householder:

proposing to a bad woman,
serving a bad chief,
exchanging for bad land.

Three excellent things for a householder:

proposing to a good woman,
serving a good chief,
exchanging for good land.

Three things which justice demands:

judgement,

measure,

conscience.

Three things which judgement demands:

wisdom,
penetration,
knowledge.

Three things for which an enemy is loved:

wealth,
beauty,
worth.

Three things for which a friend is hated:

trespassing,
keeping aloof,
fecklessness.

Three rude ones of the world:

a youngster mocking an old man,
a healthy person mocking an invalid,
a wise man mocking a fool.

Three sparks that kindle love:

a face,
demeanour,
speech.

Three deposits with usufruct:

depositing a woman,
a horse,
salt.

Three glories of the gathering:

    a beautiful wife,
    a good horse,
    a swift hound.

Three ungentlemanly things:

interrupting stories,
a mischievous game,
jesting so as to raise a blush.

Three smiles that are worse than sorrow:

the smile of the snow as it melts,
the smile of your wife on you
after another man has been with her,
the grin of a hound ready to leap at you.

Three fewnesses that are better than plenty:

a fewness of fine words,
a fewness of cows in grass,
a fewness of friends around ale.

Three laughing-stocks of the world:

an angry man,
a jealous man,
a niggard.

Three ruins of a tribe:

a lying chief,
a false judge,
a lustful priest.

Three preparations of a good man's house:

ale,
a bath,
a large fire.

Three characteristics of obstinacy:

long visits,
staring,
constant questioning.

Three signs of a fop:

the track of his comb in his hair,
the track of his teeth in his food,
the track of his stick behind him.

Three maidens that bring love to good fortune:

silence,
diligence,
sincerity.

Three maidens that bring hatred upon misfortune:

talking,
laziness,
insincerity.

The three chief sins:

avarice,
gluttony,
lust.

Three things that constitute a buffoon:

blowing out his cheek,
blowing out his satchel,
blowing out his belly.

Three things that constitute a harper:

a tune to make you cry,
a tune to make you laugh,
a tune to put you to sleep.

Three drops of a wedded woman:

a drop of blood,
a tear-drop,
a drop of sweat.

Three false sisters:

'perhaps',
'maybe',
'I dare say'.

Three sounds of increase:

the lowing of a cow in milk,
the din of a smithy,
the swish of a plough.

Three things by which
every angry person is known:

an outburst of passion,
trembling,
growing pale.

Three things that characterise
every patient person:

repose,
silence,
blushing.

Three signs of folly:

contention,
wrangling,
attachment to everybody.

Three candles that illumine every darkness:

truth,

nature,

knowledge.

Three things that make a fool wise:

learning,
steadiness,
docility.

Three things that make a wise man foolish:

quarrelling,

anger,

drunkenness.

Three things that show every good man:

a special gift,
valour,
piety.

Three things that show a bad man:

bitterness,
hatred,
cowardice.

Three things that constitute a king:

a contract with other kings,
the feast of Tara,
abundance during his reign.

Three inheritances that are divided
in the presence of heirs:

the inheritance of a jester,
of a madman,
and of an old man.

Three youthful sisters:

desire,
beauty,
generosity.

Three great rushes:

The rush of water,
The rush of fire,
The rush of falsehood.

Three woman-days:

Monday,
Tuesday,
Wednesday.

If women go to men on those days, the men will love them better than they the men, and the women will survive the men.

Three man-days:

Thursday,

Friday,

Sunday.

If women go to men on those days, they will not be loved, and their husbands will survive them. Saturday, however, is a common day. It is equally lucky to them. Monday is a free day to undertake any business.

Three things that are undignified for everyone:

driving one's horse before one's lord
so as to soil his dress,
going to speak to him without being summoned,
staring in his face as he is eating his food.

Three welcomes of an ale-house:

plenty,
kindliness,
art.

Three whose spirits are highest:

a young scholar after having read his psalms,
a youngster who has put on a man's attire,
a maiden who has been made a woman.

Three prohibitions of food:

to eat it without giving thanks,
to eat it before its proper time,
to eat it after a guest.

Three things that are best for a chief:

justice,
peace,
an army.

Three things that are worst for a chief:

sloth,
treachery,
evil counsel.

Three indications of dignity in a person:

a fine figure,
a fine bearing,
eloquence.

Three coffers whose depth is not known:

the coffer of a chieftain,
of the Church,
of a privileged poet.

Three disagreeable things at home:

a scolding wife,
a squalling child,
a smokey chimney.

The three finest sights in the world:

a field of ripe wheat,
a ship in full sail,
and the wife of a MacDonnell with child.

Acknowledgements

Irish Blessings **by Pat Fairon**

For my father and mother. With grateful thanks to Dharmuid Ó Laoghaire for permission to draw my choice of prayers and blessings from his book *Ár bPaidreacha Dúchais* where most of these prayers and blessings are to be found in their original language—Gaelic. My thanks also to Pádraig Ó hAdhmaill for ensuring that so little was lost in their translation. Thanks also to Gill and Macmillan, Dublin, for permission to reproduce prayers from Douglas Hyde's *Religious Songs of Connacht,* 1906.

Irish Toasts

For permission to reproduce copyright material the following acknowledgements are made: to Irish Distillers' Limited for a selection of ten toasts from *Sláinte!* © Irish Distillers Group Limited 1980; to Brendan Kennelly for *Saint Brigid's Prayer;* to the Head of the Department of Irish Folklore, University College, Dublin for Niall Ó Dubhthaigh's story and for the English translation to the Mercier Press (Irish Life and Lore, Seamus Ó Catháin, Mercier Press, 1982); also to Dr. Ó Catháin for translations of the four toasts on pages 82, 94, 97 and 106 (Irish Life and Lore).

Irish Riddles by Pat Fairon

For permission to reproduce material the following acknowledgements are made: The Head of the Department of Irish
Folklore, University College, Dublin, for material from
Schools Manuscripts; the Secretary of the Folklore of Ireland
Society, Dublin, for material from the journal *Bealoideas*; and
the County Museum, Armagh, for material from the Patter-
son Collection.